TEACHERS' MESSAGES AND NOTES HOME

Notes, Letters, and Messages to Parents

Laurie Steding

Troll Associates

This edition published in 2001.

Interior Illustrations by Mary Gwen Connelly

ISBN: 0-8167-3277-9
Printed in the United States of America
10 9 8 7 6 5 4 3

CONTENTS

INTRODUCTION

Mrs. Morrison is the mother of third-grader Lorna. Every morning Mrs. Morrison wakes her daughter, serves breakfast to her family, helps her youngster dress and pack her book bag, and drives Lorna to school. On the way, they talk about Lorna's classmates, her teacher, and her schoolwork. But because Mrs. Morrison is at the office all day and, in fact, gets home well after her daughter has finished her homework, she really is not sure how well her daughter is doing in class. Although she knows Lorna is reading on grade level, she'd also like to know if there's any way she can help her daughter at home, especially on weekends. Is Lorna getting along with her classmates? How's her math? Are her science projects okay? What areas of her schoolwork could use a boost? Does the class as a whole need any inexpensive art supplies she could donate? Mrs. Morrison wishes she could drop by class to chat with the teacher, even for a minute, but in her rush to get to work, it's not really possible.

This is where **Teachers' Messages and Notes Home: Notes, Letters, and Messages to Parents** comes in handy. Filled with messages, notes, certificates, and forms, the book is designed to help you, the teacher, develop a positive partnership with your students' parents. It suggests words, phrases, simple awards, and notes that will help you keep parents informed of their child's progress, in areas from classroom behavior to reading, from science to music and art. It will help you communicate with parents more frequently and succinctly because it provides easily adaptable messages that describe many areas of your students' school life.

Of course, you will need to modify the messages to suit your students' individual profiles. Every child is unique, and the words and phrases should be adapted accordingly. When writing a report card, for example, you may want to read through all the "reading" sentences in a section of this book, then create an individual report for a child.

The suggestions in this book may trigger other ideas that you hadn't thought to comment on, but which may be of importance. For example, you may not have thought to comment on a child's artwork or leadership skills. Glancing at suggested comments in **Teachers' Messages and Notes Home** may remind you of other subjects to bring to parents' attention.

Teachers' Messages and Notes Home: Notes, Letters, and Messages to Parents also contains reproducible sheets informing parents of parent/teacher meetings, class trips, behavior patterns, and more. And it will help you keep parents informed about special events—from parties to conferences—and provide a simple way to enlist their support.

All parents and teachers want children to succeed in school. **Teachers' Messages and Notes Home** will help you pool resources with parents, open communication, and increase parental involvement. The concern you show through the notes, messages, and certificates in this book can inspire parents to become partners with you in their child's education. Together, you can make a difference in each youngster's life.

CLASSROOM BEHAVIOR

Excellent Progress

_____ has been voted class president. Her classmates look up to her and admire her!

What a responsible student _____ is! She has a positive attitude toward school, and her enthusiasm motivates others around her.

_____ is independent and self-directed. Other students look to him for ideas and leadership.

Your child is diligent in listening and following directions. It makes such a difference in her academic performance!

The students and I appreciate _____ 's cheerful attitude and sense of humor. We look forward to seeing his smile every day.

Your child is such a thoughtful student! He catches on quickly to what's expected and helps others understand what to do.

Your child is socially gifted. Her classmates gravitate toward her both in the classroom and at recess. She shows thoughtfulness and sensitivity to all, and other children like to be around her.

_____ is a most thoughtful and considerate child. She gets along well with everyone.

I'm impressed with _____ 's self-control. She is patient and accepting with the other children.

Good/Fair Progress

_____ is organized and orderly. He follows all classroom rules and inspires others to do so, too. Occasionally he expresses frustration when something doesn't go the way he had hoped.

_____ is a very bright student, but he sometimes uses his abilities to interpret the class rules to fit his own needs. Let's work together to improve his acceptance of positive school behavior.

On some days _____ works hard at being a good citizen, and other days it seems she has forgotten the rules. Please call me so we can discuss how we can help her to be more consistent.

Your son requires extra guidance to follow instructions. Let's work on developing some signals to help remind him both at school and at home. Let's start with _____.

Your daughter has been trying hard lately to follow classroom regulations. Let's work together on strengthening this positive behavior. I'm sending home a list of school policies so that we can both review them with her on a regular basis.

Some days your youngster seems drowsy in class and shows less than her usual interest in lessons and activities. I wonder if she is getting to bed early enough. Let's set up a time to meet about this. I certainly want your daughter to enjoy school and learn as much as possible.

Changing _____ 's seat in class has had a positive effect on his work! He's much more focused now. Thanks for your suggestion.

Now that your child is the monitor of the class pet, I've noticed an improvement in his attitude and behavior. I hope this continues, even when the job is rotated at the end of the month.

Thank you for taking the time to see me the other day. I think the course of action we discussed is proving to be quite successful with _____. I can already see some changes in his attitude. He seems much happier and gets along better with his classmates. Keep me posted on how things are going at home, and I'll continue to send you reports.

Poor Progress/Needs Improvement

While your child is progressing in the areas of _____ and _____, he/she is having difficulty adjusting to our class routines. He/She shows uncertainty by _____. Is something going on at home that may be adversely affecting his/her behavior? Please call me to discuss this further.

_____ has been spending time in (trouble, detention, time out) with the teachers and/or other students. He needs our help to turn his behavior around. Does he have a special interest, hobby, or skill that he can share with others in class? This may gain him more positive attention in class. Please let me know a convenient time for us to discuss this.

Thank you for coming to our recent parent/teacher conference. As we discussed, _____ is grasping academic information quite easily. He does not give the same attention to his behavior. I will be sending home a daily report for you to sign. It will include a "happy face" if his behavior for the day was good, and an "unhappy face" if his behavior was poor. Please discuss these reports with your child.

I'm sure you know that I want the best for your child. I'm sorry to report that your youngster has been misbehaving in class. Please let me know when you can come to school to discuss ways to help your youngster cooperate in class.

I know _____ wants to be liked and accepted, but she is having difficulty getting along with other children. She is displaying signs of anger and seems quite unhappy. What do you think is causing her to feel this way? I would like to discuss this issue with you as soon as possible.

GOOD NEWS!

_____

has shown great citizenship in the classroom

during this grading period.

I am proud of your child.

_____
Teacher's signature

_____
Date

KEEP IT UP!

_____

has shown terrific improvement in

_____ .

I am proud of your youngster!

_____   _____
Date   Teacher's signature

SOMETHING SPECIAL!

_____

did something special in class today. He/She

_____

_____ .

I hope you're as proud of your son/daughter as I am.

_____   _____
Date   Teacher's signature

In-Class Problem Note

Date _____

Dear_____,

I want your child to shine in school. But your child is having difficulty

with_____

Specifically, he/she _____

_____

I would like for us to work together to help your child improve in this area.

Please discuss this with your child. Then sign the form below and return it to

me. I welcome your comments.

Sincerely,

_____

Teacher's signature

Parent's Comments:

_____

_____

_____

Sincerely,

_____   _____

Date   Parent's signature

Out-of-Class Problem Note

_____
Date

Dear Parents,

Your child, _____, needs help in following

directions and rules in the:

library ___   cafeteria ___   playground ___   hall ___   other _____

The difficulty arises when _____

_____

The school expects your child to _____

_____

Would you discuss this with your child? By working as a team, we can

guide your child to succeed in all areas of school.

Thank you for your cooperation.

Sincerely,

_____
Teacher's signature

Classroom Rules Letter

_____
Date

Dear Parents,

The children in class _____ have been discussing the importance of rules, and together we have decided on the following for our classroom:

1. _____

2. _____

3. _____

4. _____

5. _____

Please keep these guidelines in a safe place and go over them with your child often to make sure they are well understood. Sign the bottom portion of this form and ask your child to do the same. Your youngster should return the form to me.

Thank you for your support. Your child will benefit as a result of parents and teachers working together.

Sincerely,

_____
Teacher's signature

- -

To the Teacher:

My child, _____, and I have reviewed the rules for student

behavior in class _____.

Student's signature _____Parent's signature _____

Date_____

Daily Behavior Report

Child's Name _____

Class _____

Date _____

Code

:) = good behavior today

:(= poor behavior today

Teacher's comments

_____

_____

Teacher's signature _____

Parent's comments _____

_____

Parent's signature _____

Student's signature _____

Student's comments _____

Weekly Behavior Report

Child's Name _____ Class _____

Week Ending _____

(+) = outstanding

(√) = satisfactory

(x) = improvement needed

Behavior

___ Pays attention

___ Listens carefully

___ Respects equipment and materials

___ Works independently

___ Finishes assignments

___ Respects teachers

___ Gets along with other students

___ Follows directions

Teacher's comments

_____

_____

_____   _____

Signature   Date

Parent's comments

_____

_____

_____   _____

Signature   Date

ATTENDANCE AND PUNCTUALITY

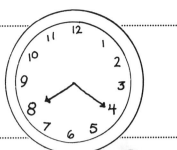

Excellent Progress

Since the beginning of the school year, _____ has always arrived to class on time. I'm glad he has developed this habit.

I'm happy to report that your child is punctual in the mornings and at lunchtime.

Your child has had 100% attendance since the beginning of school. That is a wonderful record!

Good/Fair Progress

I'm happy to say that your child has improved in punctuality. Although she was late five times last month, she has only been late once this month. Let's aim for perfect punctuality next month.

Since the last report card, your child has made good progress in her attendance record.

Poor Progress/Needs Improvement

_____ often misses the morning language arts lesson because of her lateness. Let's work together to improve her punctuality.

I'm concerned about your child's health. She has been absent ____ times in the last month. Let's meet to discuss this.

The school requires a doctor's note every time your child is absent. Could you please take your child to a physician to find out the cause of her frequent absences?

_____ is always on time in the morning. But he frequently returns to school late after lunch. _____ says he doesn't know why this happens. Let's meet to find out the reason.

BRAVO!

_____

has had 100% attendance this month.

Congratulations!

Date _____   Teacher's signature

KEEP IT UP!

_____

has shown 100% punctuality this month.

We are proud of your youngster!

Date _____   Teacher's signature

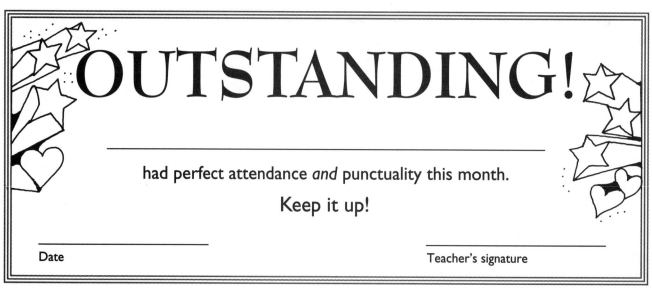

OUTSTANDING!

_____

had perfect attendance *and* punctuality this month.

Keep it up!

Date _____   Teacher's signature

READING

Excellent Progress

Your child sets a good example with her variety of reading interests. Many children have been motivated to read books based on her enthusiastic reviews.

Since _____ has developed an interest in _____, he has chosen to read many books dealing with that subject. His eagerness to read is having a dramatic effect on his confidence and skills in reading in general.

_____ prefers reading factual books and has acquired a broad storehouse of knowledge. The class enjoys his sharing of information through discussion and projects.

I'm impressed with _____'s ability to read new and difficult words. She often figures them out from the context of the story.

Listening to _____ read aloud is a joy. Her fluency is excellent, and her expressive voice makes stories "come alive."

Accuracy is very important to your child. His ability to read and follow written directions is superior.

———————————

Your youngster's comprehension is excellent. She makes good inferences about each character's behavior and enjoys sharing her interesting viewpoints with others in her reading group.

———————————

From the ease with which _____ relates events in her life to storybook characters and situations, it is easy to see that reading is valued in your home. Thank you for bringing the joy of reading into her life.

———————————

_____ reads in her spare time. She is developing a lifelong interest in books.

Good/Fair Progress

Your child enjoys her daily reading group meetings. She reads on grade level and is progressing nicely. I'm trying to encourage her to read books independently, too.

———————————

I hope your child will consider more challenging reading material. When we visit the school library, I try to encourage her to take harder books. Perhaps you can do the same when you visit your local library.

_____ is making steady progress in reading. I'm working to further develop his research skills by urging him to locate information on his own, instead of relying on others. I think some independent time at the library would be of great benefit to your son.

Your youngster enjoys sharing stories she's read with the class. Sometimes she even acts them out with friends. I'm glad to see that she likes to read.

_____'s reading comprehension is improving. If she practices at home, it will help to increase her fluency.

Today your daughter and I met to listen to two audiotapes she's made this year: one of her reading at the beginning of the year; the other of her reading mid-year. We both agree that she is becoming stronger in reading. We are happy with her progress.

In our reading conference today, your daughter, _____, mentioned that her favorite types of books are _____ (mysteries, science fiction, fantasy, animal stories, etc.), and her favorite author is _____. I am happy with her interest in books.

Poor Progress/Needs Improvement

To encourage your child to read more, consider making a motivation chart at home. She earns a star for reading a book and is rewarded when she reaches a certain number of stars. Call me for more details.

Although he enjoys the stories we've been studying, I believe _____ is struggling with the grade-level reading program. His vocabulary does not seem to be increasing at the same rate as the difficulty of the material. I'm going to send home a list of words he needs to know. Five or ten minutes of "word discussion time" every night would help your son remember the words. (You can make it into a game.) I will be happy to share some other ideas about how to improve his vocabulary at home.

As we discussed last week, your child is having difficulty in reading. This week I tried having him dictate stories to me that he has made up. He reads them back to me the next day. He underlines words he's still not sure of, then we go over them together. I'm hoping that this will help him to develop his reading skills.

A child from an older grade has volunteered to read with your youngster twice a week. They have already met once and hit it off quite well. I'm hoping that this will encourage your child to enjoy reading aloud.

With your permission, I have referred your child for testing with the school reading specialist. I've noticed that she reverses letters in her writing. This may be affecting her reading, too. I'll let you know the results of the tests as soon as they are available. We can then develop a plan to help her improve her skills.

You've mentioned that your child does not enjoy reading at home. Try going to the library and taking out some books that relate to his interests. For example, I know your son likes sports. Point out some good biographies on baseball heroes and basketball stars. These books for young readers may spark his interest.

Reading At Home With Your Child

Dear Parents:

Like most parents, you're probably looking for ways to encourage your child to read more. You know that reading for fun is a wonderful activity that contributes to overall reading ability and to success in school. Here are some ideas for increasing your child's reading ability:

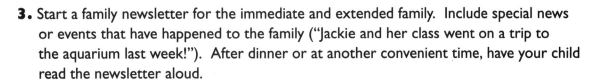

1. Read aloud to your child for 15 minutes every day. Stop at several points in the story and ask your child what he thinks will happen next.

2. Get your child his own library card. Take him to the public library at least once a month.

3. Start a family newsletter for the immediate and extended family. Include special news or events that have happened to the family ("Jackie and her class went on a trip to the aquarium last week!"). After dinner or at another convenient time, have your child read the newsletter aloud.

4. Establish a family reading time where everyone (including Mom and Dad) spends 15-30 minutes reading.

5. Ask family members to listen to your child read aloud while they are cooking, cleaning, driving, or relaxing.

6. The car is a good place for you to practice reading skills with your children. Have them read signs, billboards, and other words around them. On car trips, play such word games as rhyming and spelling.

7. Read *with* your child. Alternate listening to your child read a page or paragraph with you reading a page or paragraph.

8. Have a reading party and invite children from the neighborhood. Ask each guest to dress as a character from their favorite book.

Happy Reading!

Sincerely,

Keeping Track Of Reading

To the Student:

The more you read, the better you will get at reading. Pick a book that looks good to you. With a parent or by yourself, read for about 15 minutes every weekday evening and at least 30 minutes on the weekend. Each night, write down the name of your book(s) and the number of pages you read. At the end of the week, have a parent sign the form below. Bring a copy of this form back to class every Monday.

DAY	TITLE OF BOOK	PAGES READ
Monday	_____	_____
Tuesday	_____	_____
Wednesday	_____	_____
Thursday	_____	_____
Friday	_____	_____
Saturday	_____	_____
Sunday	_____	_____

Sincerely,

_____

Teacher's signature

- -

To the Teacher:
This week my child read at least 15 minutes each weeknight and at least 30 minutes over the weekend.

Sincerely,

_____

Parent's signature

Week Ending _____

LANGUAGE ARTS

Excellent Progress

Your child is respectful and an attentive listener. He knows how to make others feel good about their reports and stories.

_____

The class loves all the interesting books and articles that _____ brings from home to supplement our units of study. Her interest in and extensions of our projects are very positive influences on others.

_____

I enjoy seeing the poise _____ shows when speaking before the class. He always has something interesting to say.

_____

_____ made a wonderful presentation of her project on _____. I was impressed by the way she gathered and organized her information.

_____

Your child has been writing some interesting entries in his journal lately. He has shown much thought and sensitivity in his writing.

What an imagination _____ has! Her stories are always original and compelling. _____ is a very talented child.

_____'s ability to reason and express his thoughts in writing is delightful. Not only do I think he is a gifted writer, but I recommend that we explore ways to submit some of his work for possible publication in children's magazines. Let's talk about this at our next meeting.

Your child won the class spelling bee! I'm not s-u-r-p-r-i-s-e-d!

Your child's favorite author is _____. She is using that author as a model for her own writing.

Good/Fair Progress

Your child has strong verbal skills. He expresses his ideas very clearly when talking. We need to encourage him to express his thoughts more clearly in writing.

Your child has a nice way of putting words on paper. We are now concentrating on giving a little more attention to the appearance of her work. She has been pleased at how many errors she has been able to edit herself. Let's continue to work with her in this area at home and at school.

_____ begins with fine, original ideas for his writing. I'm seeing signs of frustration, though, because his papers often end up lacking direction and support for his great plans. Perhaps through a parent/student/teacher conference, we can show him some ways to help him improve his outlining and other pre-writing skills. Call me to set up a time to meet.

Poor Progress/Needs Improvement

_____ has some good ideas for writing, but we need to plan ways to provide your child with some extra help in spelling and punctuation. Please come by or call me for a conference.

_____ is having difficulty concentrating on his writing. Perhaps as a threesome, we can help your child come up with topic choices that he'll want to write about. Please call me as soon as possible to set up a time for our conference.

Your child tells spirited, interesting anecdotes in class, but is not able to convey those thoughts on paper. I am working with her in this area.

Your child is having difficulty with her handwriting. I'm sending home a handwriting book, which she can use to practice. Will you help me by working with her at home?

Your child may need some special help with her speech. Please see me regarding arrangements to test her.

We need to pool our resources in helping _____ to distinguish similarities and differences in words she writes. I think with some reminders and some games, both at school and at home, we can really make progress.

Thank you for taking the time to observe _____ in a classroom situation. As we discussed, she needs some extra help with _____. Let's get together in a month or so to evaluate her progress.

SOCIAL STUDIES

Excellent Progress

_____ makes great contributions to our discussions in social studies. He has especially interesting things to say about _____.

I like how your child draws parallels between historical events and current events.

Your child is well informed about current events. You must have many interesting family discussions.

Your child has good insight into political issues.

_____ has become fascinated with maps. He spends much of his free time looking at or drawing them.

We were impressed when _____ shared his volunteer work with us last week. He is proving to be a good example to his classmates.

I'm pleased with the way _____ has combined math concepts with social studies in his reports. The charts and graphs he produces are dazzling.

Good/Fair Progress

Your child is confused about the difference between countries and cities. Perhaps you can supplement my classroom instruction by going over the difference with him. I've attached a map of the world.

In social studies class, we have been studying how a coat is made. Attached are puppets showing people involved in the different stages of manufacturing, from farmer/shearer to weaver to store owner. To reinforce learning, please allow your child to re-enact the story for your family. It will be educational and entertaining for your child.

Your child is studying the theme of _____ in social studies. Can you help your youngster look through old magazines and newspapers to find articles related to this subject?

Your child's social studies project on _____ is due on _____. Please help him ration his time so the completed project meets our deadline.

We have found an interesting way to help you know what your child is studying in social studies. Starting this week, your youngster will write a weekly letter to you describing his social studies activities. Please read his letter and write comments in the appropriate place. I will initial the letter, too. This way you will continue to be informed about his progress. By the way, he's doing fine!

Poor Progress/Needs Improvement

_____ is working to learn about authority and responsibility in government. He is becoming a better classroom citizen by applying his knowledge.

We are working with your child on becoming more familiar with geographical terms. I will send home a list of words for you to use when you work with her at home. Thank you for your interest.

I agree with your concern about your daughter's social studies grade. It may help _____ learn the concepts in her social studies book if she reads a few pages with you every night and briefly reviews the previous night's work.

_____ works very hard to memorize the facts learned both in class and in books. We are working with him to consider "why" and "how" the facts came to be so that he will have a true picture of history. I will send home a list of concepts we're studying. It would help him to participate in some family discussions.

Your child receives satisfactory grades in social studies. But he has trouble understanding and accepting points of view other than his own. I will be happy to give you a list of books you can read at home which may increase his sensitivity toward others.

Although your daughter participates in class discussions about social studies con-cepts, she is having difficulty understanding the relationships between times and places. It would help if you can work with her at home to construct a time line and a map for each of our units. I think that will improve her understanding.

MATH

Excellent Progress

Your child excels in math. He is especially talented in problem solving. I recommend that he be tested for entry into a special math program for gifted and talented students. Please call me if you agree to pursue the testing.

Incorporating math into daily life comes naturally to _____. She is able to help others understand math problems by giving relevant examples. I can tell that you must be a math-oriented family. Thank you for your child's preparation and your participation.

_____ is making tremendous progress in interpreting data from graphs and other pictorial representations. He's been spending much of his spare time working on tables and charts and organizing numbers. I'm thrilled by his interest and by his achievement.

I'm impressed with the speed with which _____ recalls her math facts. She learned them quickly, as well.

Your child has fallen in love with the computer. He has shown such interest that he elects to use the computer area during all of his free time. I suggest he join our after school computer club. Call me for details if you're interested.

It is easy to see that _____ has been interested in money for some time. She is inspiring other children to count and sort money for all sorts of reasons. _____ is a strong math student.

_____ is extremely good at solving problems with logic, and he has developed quite an ability to construct models of mathematical ideas. We are all proud of him.

I am impressed with your child's flexibility with numbers.

Good/Fair Progress

From _____'s math journal I see that he enjoys the subject. He explains his math reasoning in his writing.

On our math facts practice tests, your child consistently scores near 100 percent. I can tell you've been working with him. Now that he's doing so well with his facts, let's begin working with him on applying his knowledge to word problems. You can make word problems out of everyday situations at home. Call me for some ideas.

_____ has good "math sense," but needs to master the math facts. I am steering him towards the math games in the classroom to reinforce learning.

There has been noticeable improvement in _____ 's work; she is applying formulas well in solving difficult equations. Now we need to help her work on her estimation and prediction skills. Please stop in for a list of games and ideas for estimating at home the way we do in class.

_____ appears to be a very competent math student, both in classwork and in home-work. None of his test scores, however, reflect his abilities. I've been talking to him, but we need to work as a team to lick this problem. If you call me, I will be happy to share some ideas to relieve test anxiety.

Your child is working so hard to achieve accuracy with math! Unfortunately, his speed is suffering because he is afraid to make a mistake. Let's help him relax and enjoy math more. I have some games which I would be glad to lend you, if you are interested.

Poor Progress/Needs Improvement

Thank you for talking with me about your son's math work. Although I moved his seat to a less distracting location, _____ is not able to concentrate. Let's start by having him work 15 minutes a day with an older student for some extra math attention and see if his work improves. We don't want to put too much pressure on him, but there are some things you can make a game out of, so that he doesn't realize you're doing math! Please see me for a list of "sneaky" math ideas.

I know you're concerned about your daughter's progress in math. _____ doesn't appear to relate the math symbols to their functions. I've been working individually with her, but I think she needs some extra attention. I will call you next week to hear your ideas.

Last time we talked you voiced concern about your son's math grades. Has anything been said at home? I'm concerned that _____ has lost confidence in his ability to solve math problems. We need to bring a lot of everyday math into his world so he can feel comfortable once again. I have a book about this. Would you like to borrow it? Please see me as soon as possible.

When we are learning something new in math class, your child follows along well and seems to understand the concepts taught. However, this is not reflected in her homework. Can you spare an extra ten minutes every night? I will jot down the lessons we cover in class; you can reinforce them at home before she begins her homework.

In our previous talks, you've mentioned the time and effort you've spent working with your daughter in math. I share your concern; _____ is not grasping the required math concepts at our grade level despite the extra help I've been giving her. I recommend that she have some testing done in this area to see what is interfering with her learning. Please write me back with your comments.

Math Activities For The Home (Grades K-3) Letter

Dear Parents:

Like most parents, you're probably looking for ways to encourage your grades K-3 child to become better in math. Did you know that activities around the house are often a good source of informal mathematics learning? You can help your youngster learn in the course of everyday events. The ideas listed here will reinforce your child's schoolwork. You can try:

- Kitchen activities ("We have five children at the kitchen table and ten cookies on the plate. If we give each child the same number of cookies, how many will each child get?") *Teaches Division*

- Counting activities ("Let's count the pennies we saved in the piggy bank. Do you think the number will be closer to two dollars or five dollars? What makes you say that?") *Teaches Estimating*

- Going shopping activities ("If we give the man a dollar, and the ice cream costs 75 cents, how much change should he give us?") *Teaches Money/Subtraction*

- Measurement activities ("Look at the new pencil mark on the wall. How many inches have you grown since the last time we measured you?") *Teaches Measurement*

- Living room activities ("Your favorite TV show starts in one hour. It's 4:00 now. What time will your show come on?") *Teaches Time*

- Clean-up activities ("Let me help you organize the toys in your room. Here are two boxes. How should we sort the toys: outside toys and inside toys? Games and dolls? Old and new?") *Teaches Sorting/Classifying*

Sincerely,

_____
Teacher's signature

Math Activities For The Home (Grades 4-6) Letter

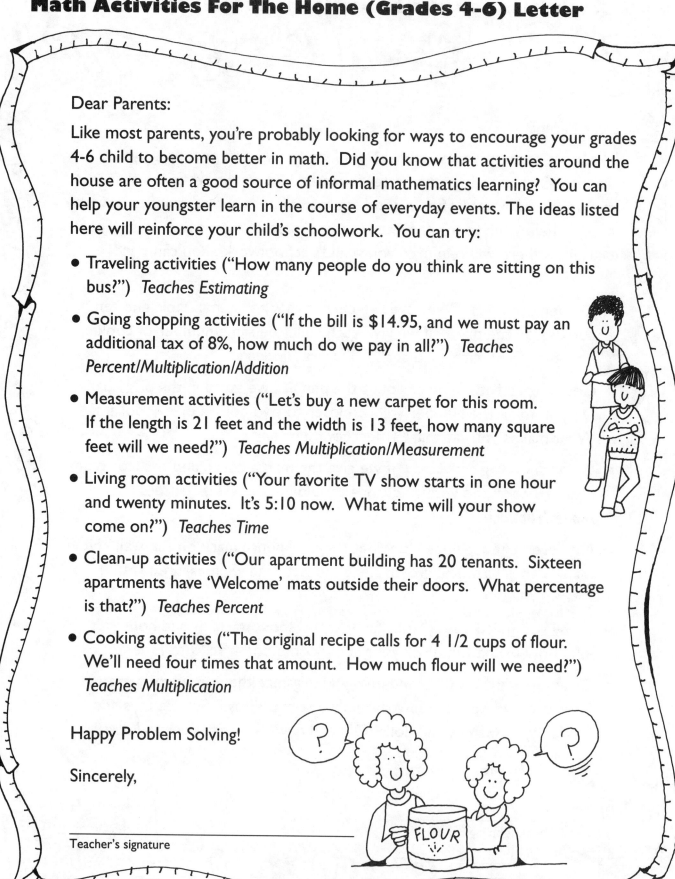

Dear Parents:

Like most parents, you're probably looking for ways to encourage your grades 4-6 child to become better in math. Did you know that activities around the house are often a good source of informal mathematics learning? You can help your youngster learn in the course of everyday events. The ideas listed here will reinforce your child's schoolwork. You can try:

- Traveling activities ("How many people do you think are sitting on this bus?") *Teaches Estimating*

- Going shopping activities ("If the bill is $14.95, and we must pay an additional tax of 8%, how much do we pay in all?") *Teaches Percent/Multiplication/Addition*

- Measurement activities ("Let's buy a new carpet for this room. If the length is 21 feet and the width is 13 feet, how many square feet will we need?") *Teaches Multiplication/Measurement*

- Living room activities ("Your favorite TV show starts in one hour and twenty minutes. It's 5:10 now. What time will your show come on?") *Teaches Time*

- Clean-up activities ("Our apartment building has 20 tenants. Sixteen apartments have 'Welcome' mats outside their doors. What percentage is that?") *Teaches Percent*

- Cooking activities ("The original recipe calls for 4 1/2 cups of flour. We'll need four times that amount. How much flour will we need?") *Teaches Multiplication*

Happy Problem Solving!

Sincerely,

_____
Teacher's signature

SCIENCE

Excellent Progress

Your child is positively wild about science!
All his spare time is devoted to reading about
or concocting experiments.

_____

I've rarely met a child more involved with science than _____. He has motivated
several classmates to do extra research and has helped raise the interest level of the
class in general.

_____

Your child has shared fascinating material for science. Her collections have attracted
the attention of most of the class. Thank you for letting the other children enjoy them.

_____

Our science curriculum this year has been very discovery oriented—exactly to _____ 's
liking. His desire for hands-on learning was well satisfied.

_____

Your child has quite a talent for observing and noting detail. Her science projects this
year were extremely thorough and well organized.

_____

_____ is especially good at predicting results from our science experiments. She always
is able to back her answers with reasonable data.

_____

_____ is developing skills in interpreting data and drawing conclusions from our scientific observations in class.

_____

Your child has expanded his understanding of math concepts through his interest in
science. He has been working on _____.

_____

_____ has a real interest in anything mechanically oriented. Her valuable service to
her science group has been much appreciated.

_____

_____ excels in science because he is so curious about everything in the world and
certainly not afraid to ask questions! We have many lively discussions based on his
inquiries.

Good/Fair Progress

I am so proud of your child's improvement in science this grading period. Her persistence in questioning and studying really paid off.

We have a number of science books in the classroom. Your child enjoys reading them as a follow-up to the science lessons.

Your child writes in a science log twice a week. In it he shows that he understands the concepts of our unit, but needs help in organizing his ideas for his final projects. I am helping him to plan his work.

_____ participates with her group in all science experiments. She seemed to especially enjoy the unit on _____.

Poor Progress/Needs Improvement

_____ has some very original ideas. Let's think of some ways to coax him to back up his scientific undertakings with numerical and factual data. I have some charts and tables I can copy for you—then he can consult them. A good gift for him would be a set of reference books.

_____ relies on others to supply him with information during group work in science. We need to help him develop more confidence in his own observations. I'm spending a little extra time with him when he's not surrounded by his science group, and I've been asking him lots of questions and waiting for him to answer. This technique would work well at home. I'll send you a list of concepts we're studying. Can we then meet in a couple of weeks to discuss progress?

Your child shows aptitude in science, but she gets a little too enthusiastic around our delicate equipment. I think a little practice at home with equipment such as glass, tweezers, teaspoons, etc., will improve her awareness and sensitivity.

ART, MUSIC, DRAMA, MOVEMENT

General Progress

Your daughter's art projects show a lot of thought and skill. She is quite talented.

_____

Your son has an eye for detail in his artwork. His drawings are wonderfully intricate.

_____

_____ has kept the class entertained with cartoon sketches of her friends.

_____

Your child has a wonderful sense of color and space in his design work.

_____

It is clear that your daughter comes from an art-loving family. Her knowledge about artists and styles of art has been informative to us all. _____'s vivid imagination is expressed well through her artwork. She is clearly looking forward to our class trip to the museum.

_____

Your child's favorite art medium is _____ (clay, watercolor, charcoal, crayon, pencil, metal, wood, cut paper). Her _____ (paintings, sculptures) are lovely and imaginative.

_____

Your child's well-developed sense of observation is evident in his art.

_____

Your daughter always has a little song for every occasion. Her tunes help cheer us up.

_____

Your son has a strong appreciation for all types of music. He is a good influence on the other children.

_____

Your child enjoys music class and has a good memory for the words and the tunes of our songs.

_____ played the piano for our class recently. It was most enjoyable for everyone. He is a fine musician.

Did you know that your child played his musical instrument for our recent assembly? Nice job!

Your child's memory served him well as he delivered his lines so expressively in our skit. He did a fantastic job! Thanks for working with him on his part.

_____'s enthusiasm for drama has gotten the whole class excited about performing for other classes.

Thanks for contributing your time and energy to our recent school play. The class and I appreciate your efforts and those of your child.

Your child shows such a flair for creative movement! Her dance interpretations are well expressed.

Art Supplies List

_____
Date

Dear Parents,

In order to express themselves during art time, the children need to use a variety of art materials. If you have any of the following items, please send them to school for the class to enjoy.

Thank you for your help!

sequins   cotton balls

fabric (large or small pieces)   wallpaper scraps

ribbon   gift wrapping paper

rickrack   lace

old magazines   old newspapers

yarn or wool   buttons

cork   string

sponges   old crayons

baby food jars, cleaned, for paints

other: _____

Sincerely,

_____
Teacher's signature

Dramatic Play Supplies List

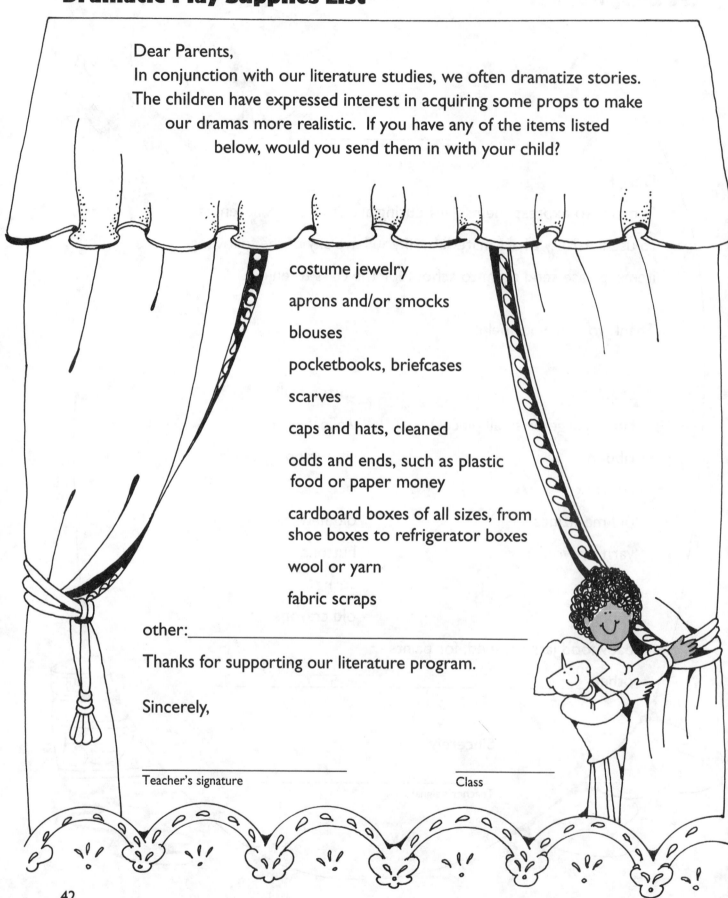

Dear Parents,

In conjunction with our literature studies, we often dramatize stories. The children have expressed interest in acquiring some props to make our dramas more realistic. If you have any of the items listed below, would you send them in with your child?

- costume jewelry
- aprons and/or smocks
- blouses
- pocketbooks, briefcases
- scarves
- caps and hats, cleaned
- odds and ends, such as plastic food or paper money
- cardboard boxes of all sizes, from shoe boxes to refrigerator boxes
- wool or yarn
- fabric scraps

other:_____

Thanks for supporting our literature program.

Sincerely,

_____
Teacher's signature

_____
Class

OTHER FORMS AND LETTERS

Trip Permission Slip

Dear Parents,

On _____ , our class will be going on a trip to

_____.

We will be leaving at _____ (time)

and arriving back at school at _____ (time).

We are traveling by: _____.

Your child needs: _____.

If you can accompany the class that day, please let me know.

Please sign the appropriate space below and have your child
return the bottom portion of this sheet to school.

- -

My child, _____ , has my permission to accompany the

class on the field trip to _____ on _____.

My child, _____ , does not have permission to accompany

the class on the field trip to _____ on _____.

_____   _____
Date   Parent's signature

Family Invitation

_____
Date

Dear Parents,
We're having a special event
in our classroom!

Activity: _____

Date: _____

Time: _____

Please join us!

Sign and return the bottom portion of this letter.

- -

YES, _____ (number of people) will attend

the special event in the classroom on _____.

NO, I/we cannot attend

the special event in the classroom on _____.

_____
Child's name

_____
Parent's signature

Parent/Teacher Conference Form

_____
Date

Dear Parents,

I invite you to visit your child's classroom for a parent/teacher conference. We will discuss your child's progress in school and you will have a chance to see some of your child's work. This is a good opportunity for us to get to know one another so that we can work together to aid your child's growth and development.

I have scheduled your conference for:

Date: _____

Time: _____ a.m.

_____ p.m.

Please sign below and return to school.

_____
Teacher's signature

To the Teacher:

I / We will attend the parent/teacher conference as scheduled.

I/We cannot attend the parent/teacher conference as scheduled.

I prefer: Date _____   Time _____

Child's name: _____

Child's class: _____

Parent's signature: _____

Parent/Teacher Conference Summary

Dear Parents,

This is a follow-up to our recent parent/teacher conference on _____ .

Child's name: _____

Parent's name: _____

Type of conference (circle):

      telephone   **in school**   **home visit**

Content of conference:

_____

_____

Parent and teacher agree:

_____

Parent and teacher disagree:

_____

Suggested action:

_____

_____

Follow-up conference:

_____

_____
Teacher's signature

School Supplies Request Letter

_____
Date

Dear Parents,

Many families ask me what school supplies their child will need this year. The checked items below reflect materials your child will need. If there is any problem in securing these items, please let me know. I will try to help.

- [ ] pencils with erasers
- [ ] crayons or non-toxic markers (thin or thick)
- [ ] colored pencils
- [ ] scissors
- [ ] paste or glue
- [ ] ruler
- [ ] scratch pad
- [ ] assignment book
- [ ] notebook
- [ ] folders
- [ ] tissues

Thanks for your help.

Sincerely,

_____
Teacher's signature

Parent Volunteers Request Letter

_____
Date

Dear Parents,

Many parents are eager to help out in class, if only for one or two visits. If you have the time, we would welcome your assistance. Please let us know which of the following areas you can assist with, and when you would be able to volunteer. If you can come on a regular basis (such as every Tuesday morning), we'd like to know that as well.

Please check those that apply.

☐ prepare learning materials (cut out materials, etc.)

☐ prepare costumes and props for a class play

☐ work with selected students in math

☐ work with selected students in reading

☐ work with selected students on the computer

☐ play instrument to accompany class

☐ help with cooking projects

☐ accompany class on field trips

☐ talk about occupation or hobby

☐ play games with students

☐ teach a dance

☐ read a story aloud to a small group

☐ videotape class activities

☐ other (specify): _____

Student's name: _____

Volunteer's name: _____

Volunteer's phone number: _____

Dates and/or times available: _____

Thanks for your help.

Sincerely,

_____
Teacher's signature